Preparing for the New Rite of Penance

A HOMILY & TEACHING GUIDE

Joseph M. Champlin

AVE MARIA PRESS / NOTRE DAME / INDIANA 46556

FATHER JOSEPH M. CHAMPLIN, former Associate Director, Secretariat, Bishops' Committee on the Liturgy, is Pastor of Holy Family Church, Fulton, New York. He has lectured extensively throughout the country, and his syndicated column appears in 90 Catholic newspapers.

In addition to *Together in Peace*—the most complete priest/penitent study guide available for the celebration of the new Rite of Penance—he is the author of *Together for Life,* a popular marriage preparation book which has sold over one million copies, also, *Don't You Really Love Me?* (200,000 in print), *Christ Present and Yet to Come, The Mass in a World of Change,* and *The Sacraments in a World of Change.* Father Champlin has also appeared on national radio and television, and has recorded a number of cassettes on liturgy and pastoral life.

Acknowledgment

English translation of excerpts from the *Rite of Penance,* copyright © 1974, International Committee on English in the Liturgy, Inc. All rights reserved.

Nihil Obstat: Rev. John L. Roark
              Censor Deputatus
              July 31, 1975

Imprimatur: Most Rev. David F. Cunningham, D.D.
             Bishop of Syracuse

© 1975 by Ave Maria Press. All rights reserved

Printed in the United States of America

Preparing for the New Rite of Penance

Contents

Introduction 7

Guiding Principles 8

Homilies 12

    Homily 1 *Sin* 14

    Homily 2 *Reconciliation* 18

    Homily 3 *God's Good Words About Forgiveness* 22

    Homily 4 *Signs of Sorrow and Forgiveness* 26

    Homily 5 *A Sacrament for Growth* 32

    Homily 6 *Together in Peace* 38

Material for the Weekly Bulletin 42

Handouts 50

    Rite for Reconciliation of Individual Penitents 51

    Communal Penance Services 53

    How to Use *Together in Peace* 55

Introduction

The English translation of the revised rite of Penance has been approved by the American bishops and the Holy See. Its official implementation date has also been determined by our hierarchy with Lent, 1977 being the "must" date for its universal use on the national level.

A rather extended period thus exists between Rome's approval of the translation and the final mandated time for initiation. The National Conference of Catholic Bishops in the United States provided this interval deliberately and called upon priests and parish or worship community leaders to use the months for an intensive session of catechesis on the renewed ritual.

The material in this booklet has been designed specifically for that teaching, preaching, explaining task.

It contains: 1) Some guiding principles and practical suggestions for this catechesis on reconciliation; 2) six homilies and their detailed outlines covering pertinent topics which need to be discussed; 3) a series of paragraphs on the revised rite which may be included in the weekly bulletin; 4) three ready-to-be-copied handouts for distribution to parishioners after Masses on appropriate weekends which outline the rite of reconciliation of individual penitents, a communal penance service, and the penitent's edition of *Together in Peace*.

The priest's edition of *Together in Peace* should prove very helpful as a basic resource text in this process. References to it will be indicated in this fashion (*TIP*, p. .....).

Guiding Principles

The following general principles should be kept in mind as community leaders plan and execute the catechesis on penance:

1. "The people's understanding of church history is usually only as long as their memory." That is to say, for most lay persons in the congregation their concept of tradition in the Church is limited to what they can recall from their own earliest days.

   In many of the other liturgical changes that fact has been the source of countless anxieties and tensions. For example, persons who for many years knew only a Latin Mass, Communion when kneeling, and priests distributing the Eucharist tend to feel unconsciously that "this is the way it has always been." They think the Church has never known other procedures and thus tend to believe these methods were of divine origin. A change in the established order, therefore, causes pain and doubt. To them it appears the agent of change has attacked the very foundations of their faith.

   An explanatory filmstrip like the Alpha production, *Understanding the Liturgy,* with its clear delineation of the historical development of our worship ritual can have a tremendous impact on many parishioners. Through it, they understand in just a few moments how present innovations have deep roots in the past and often follow procedures observed in early Christian days.

   Similarly, a filmstrip like *Sinner Sam* (a TeleKETICS production from the Franciscan Communications Center in Los Angeles) can dispel considerable misunderstanding about the ritual for Penance. Viewers will note that communal penitential services have their ultimate origin in practices of the first Christian years. So-called "devotional confessions" date back to the Irish monks of the fifth-seventh centuries, and our customary confessional "boxes" became standard procedure only in the 1500's.

2. "There are two kinds of catechesis—one for the mind and the other of the heart." The former can be achieved with relative swiftness and ease; the latter requires patience and takes time.

    A homily or two easily explains a new, positive approach to Extreme Unction as the Anointing of the Sick. For Catholic persons to accept this doctrine in the heart, however, and for them to lose the "last rites" concept will demand more effort and a longer period of adjustment.

    In parallel fashion, the notions of face-to-face encounters in the sacrament of Penance, of shared biblical readings, and flexibility with regard to the act of contrition may readily be accepted by the mind. Getting the heart to endorse these innovations and translate them into practice will very likely be a quite different story.

3. "A catechesis introducing the new rite of Penance should be progressive, persuasive and gradual."

    This overriding general norm flows from the first two principles.

    The catechesis should be *progressive*.

    We belong to a pilgrim Church, a community on the move, a faith which seeks a kingdom yet to come. Christ calls us constantly to a change of heart, a "metanoia." We need, therefore, open hearts which are willing to change, to grow, to move forward, to progress, to adopt new forms.

    Not all change brings progress, but all progress necessitates change. The parish leaders, consequently, by their very positions ought to be agents of change, progressive persons who are anxious to move forward with the Church.

    The catechesis should be *persuasive*.

    Lasting change comes more from inner conviction and external persuasion than from outward commands or imperatives which force a reluctant acceptance on the part of people.

    Parish leaders, as a result, would do well to develop a catechesis which brings out the positive values and historical tradition of the revised rite for Penance. Such a soft-sell, constructive approach will, normally, win over the hearts of most people and lead them to accept the change from within.

The catechesis should be *gradual*.

Alvin Toffler's *Future Shock* offers real insight for parish leaders in this regard. His very popular text (now in paperback) documents the effect of rapid change upon people. It is not change, even radical change, that upsets a person; rather, it is the rate of change which troubles the individual.

A catechesis on Penance, therefore, ought to be spread over a lengthy period, probably six months to a year at least. After each presentation (homily, lecture, class, flyer handout, bulletin paragraph), there should be an interval for absorption and adjustment. This enables the hearer or reader consciously and unconsciously to accept in gradual fashion the new, different approach and then move to a next level of change.

Parish leaders may find that introducing parts of the new ritual on a gradual basis instead of implementing the whole rite on a given date may prove effective. The new absolution formula, the reading of scripture, the act of contrition are examples of separate entities which could be initiated one by one after the necessary catechesis on a specific weekend. That immediate "doing after hearing" has a certain value to it.

This gradual implementation will not eliminate all tensions and dissipate every hostility, but it will substantially reduce them.

4. "The catechesis for the new rite of Penance requires a multilevel approach."

Sunday homily time represents the prime occasion for an explanation of the revised ritual. These are the moments when we have the greatest number of people present and when most parishioners assemble for a given event. Thus, this booklet includes six homilies for that purpose and a list of Sundays when these sermons would be appropriate.

The Sunday *bulletin* forms an extension, as it were, of the homily. A paragraph inserted there every other week or two could help prepare for or build upon the spoken word. We have included a series of brief notes suitable for such insertion in the weekly handout.

Religion class for Catholic and public school students offers an excellent opportunity for a deeper, more thorough study of the renewed text. The priest's edition for the instructor and the penitent's issue for the students of *Together in Peace* should be helpful as a basic text. Topics covered in a cursory way by the homily can be treated more thoroughly in the classroom environment.

Sessions for *parents* preparing children for First Penance provide a natural context for explaining the various aspects of the reformed rite. Again, the instructor should find *TIP,* the priest's edition, useful in this regard, with parents following along in the penitent's version.

Small group study sessions offer those interested an opportunity to learn about and discuss in detail the ritual and *TIP*'s five-step process for implementation of the rite.

Preparation for the *sacrament itself* may indirectly teach people about the reformed liturgy for Penance. Copies of the penitent's edition of *TIP* placed near a confessional or reconciliation room will encourage persons waiting for the priest to read through the booklet. This, in turn, can turn for them an uncomfortable, wasted period of delay into disposition-building, scripture-oriented, prayer-filled moments of preparation.

Homilies

This section contains six homilies which cover some of the salient points involved with the new rite for Penance. Presumably they would be delivered at intervals over a period of time on six Sundays according to the schedule provided in this booklet.

The author presents them with certain reservations. A good homily should be extremely personal and come from the preacher's own heart. Using (worse, reading) another's text fails in that regard and seriously weakens the impact of any sermon.

Consequently, after each homily is a rather detailed outline of the preceding sermon. This writer hopes that preachers will first read through the homily itself and then, aided by the outline, develop their own messages.

Homily 1—Sin   p. 14

2—Reconciliation   p. 18

3—God's Good Words About Forgiveness   p. 22

4—Signs of Sorrow and Forgiveness   p. 26

5—A Sacrament for Growth   p. 32

6—Together in Peace   p. 38

SUGGESTED HOMILY SCHEDULE

Originally I had intended to present here a list of Sundays from September, 1975, through September, 1976, which contained at least one scriptural reading from which an explanatory homily would flow rather naturally.

However, in researching those Sundays and their readings we discovered almost every weekend could be satisfactorily used as an occasion to cover one of the six homily topics.

To illustrate:

> Series A—23rd Sunday in Ordinary Time
> Suitable for Homily 1 on "Sin"
>
> September 14—Feast of the Triumph of the Cross
> Suitable for Homily 3—"God's Good Words About Forgiveness"
> and for Homily 4—"Signs of Sorrow and Forgiveness"
>
> Series A—25th and 26th Sundays in Ordinary Time
> Both suitable for Homily 2—"Reconciliation" and Homily 3
>
> Series A—27th Sunday in Ordinary Time
> Suitable for Homily 5—"A Sacrament for Growth" and
> Homily 6—"Together in Peace"

Some Sundays, of course, lend themselves much more effectively and obviously to the task and the topic. But most, with some planning and imagination, can serve as appropriate weekends for the needed catechesis.

It does not seem wise to alter the Sunday cycle of readings and replace them with passages specifically designed for the particular homily.

Our suggestion, therefore, is to plan in a general way the time schedule for these six homilies and then with lectionary in hand select the exact Sunday or weekend which contains scriptural readings you think best fit the designated topic.

Homily 1   Sin

A young college student kissed her parents farewell at the entrance to the airport's security clearance apparatus. She then half-shouted some excited final instructions:

"When I get there, I will put in a person-to-person call to myself at the home number. You just say I am not there and then you will know I have arrived at school."

Does that sound familiar? Do you see anything wrong in her behavior? Would you say she sinned?

How about this one:

A factory worker says to his wife: "Call the plant and tell them I'm sick. It is such a fine day I am going hunting with some buddies." She follows his wishes. The foreman, hearing this, tells a worker on the previous shift he will have to stay on for another shift even though it costs the company time-and-a-half wages.

Right or wrong behavior? Sinful or not? How would you judge his action? Hers?

Here is a final situation to think about:

You are on vacation at a special place, staying at this comfortable hotel or motel. As you prepare to leave, you say to yourself: "Of course the owners expect we will take a towel or ashtray as a souvenir."

These three incidents should bring out how we as contemporary people, as members of the modern world, tend to cover over matters, to rationalize our actions, to make excuses which justify wrong behavior.

In a recent, best-selling book the famous psychiatrist, Dr. Karl Menninger, maintains that modern men and women have lost a sense of sin.

In the book called *Whatever Became of Sin?* Dr. Menninger cites many instances to prove his point and suggests reasons for the disappearance of the word "sin" from our vocabulary.

As an illustration of the trend, the psychiatrist mentions the trial of Lt. William Calley for the killing of helpless women and babies in Vietnam. Many objected to Calley's conviction and few ever said what he did could be labeled a sin.

Menninger, however, insists people still sin. Sin, for him, should be spelled with a capital I in the middle. Sin thus means selfish behavior, behavior in which I knowingly and willingly hurt another by my aggressive behavior or injure myself by my own self-destructive behavior.

The psychiatrist likewise believes that we need today to revive or reassert the sense of personal responsibility for our actions, good or bad. While many factors do, in his opinion, diminish our responsibility, Menninger thinks we have gone too far in that direction and need to regain this sense of sin.

Dr. Menninger's position can find great support in teachings of the bible and the tradition in the Catholic Church.

Sacred scripture certainly speaks often about sin and the Church believes that Jesus came precisely to save us from our sins.

The classic biblical description of sin is contained in the third chapter of Genesis—the familiar poetic account of Adam and Eve.

These people were meant to be at peace with God, with each other, and with the world around them. But their sin ruptured all of those relationships.

After their sinful disobedience, they hid from God, felt ashamed and ultimately were expelled from the garden.

Intended to be helpmates, to be two in one flesh, they instead, after the fall or sin, quarreled and blamed each other. Adam blamed Eve, Eve blamed the serpent, and their offspring Cain killed his brother Abel.

Finally, the peaceful world of nature was disrupted by this first or original sin. In those days the primary male task was seen to be the breadwinner. Henceforth, they learned a man will earn this bread by the sweat of his brow, in hard work and difficult labor.

So, also, the primary female task was then considered to be childbearing. Eve likewise heard a promise that from this moment on women would fulfill that role with sorrow, pain and labor.

In our days those predictions continue to be fulfilled. Sin not only severs or weakens our friendship with God, it also disrupts our relationships with others and disturbs the world we live in.

The distress of Vietnam refugees and orphan babies are current examples of this. The sin of an American soldier and a Vietnamese woman has far-reaching ramifications. Just to name a few, it affects the child born, the adoptive parents in the United States, the neighbors and friends as the youngster grows older. Sin does more than cut a person off from God.

A stone dropped into a swimming pool plunges to the bottom, but the ripples caused by the rock roll to every side of the pool. A sin likewise has a far-reaching impact, touching more than our friendship with God.

But to be aware of this triple effect of sin we must have a basic sense of sin and our own sinfulness. Even more importantly, we cannot really believe that Jesus is Savior, that he will forgive and free us from our moral failures, unless we first recognize and acknowledge that we have sinned and we are sinners.

OUTLINE OF HOMILY 1

Main thought: Modern man has generally lost a sense of sin and forgotten that sin disturbs our relationship with God, one another and the world around us.

Aim of the congregation: I will seek to become more sensitive about my own sinfulness and aware of the impact my actions have on others and the world around me.

I. INTRODUCTION

   Examples of contemporary loss of sense of sin
   —Long-distance call
   —Absenteeism
   —Hotel souvenir

II. BODY

   A. *Contemporary Loss of Sense of Sin*
      —Menninger's book, *Whatever Became of Sin?* (New York: Hawthorn Books; also available in paperback)
      —Example of Calley, p. 13
      —Menninger's definition of sin, pp. 13, 18-20, 22-23
      —Need for sense of personal responsibility, p. 178
      —Need for more preaching about sin, p. 228

   B. *Triple Effect of Sin*
      —Genesis story, 3:1-19 (*TIP*, pp. 34-38)
      —Sin breaks friendship with God
      —Sin ruptures or weakens relationship with one another
      —Sin disturbs world around us
      —Orphan babies from Vietnam

III. CONCLUSION

   —Stone dropped into pool
   —To call Jesus Savior, we need to sense we are sinners.

Homily 2   Reconciliation

Perhaps you noticed recently in the bulletin and from the pulpit we have announced the hours for celebrating the sacrament of Penance would be from 4:00-5:00 and from 7:30-8:30.

Did something strike you as different? The hours are the same, of course, but instead of saying, "Confessions will be heard," we used the phrase "celebrating the sacrament of Penance."

The change is small, but significant. Throughout the United States beginning soon, Catholic parishes will start to use a new rite for confession. However, the book containing this ritual is called, not the order for confession, but the order of Penance or Rite of Reconciliation.

The term "penance" has been chosen with care. Its origin is in the Latin word, *penitentia,* or the Greek word, *metanoia.* Both mean a change of heart and the technical term "penance" includes the entire process by which a sinner changes heart, so to speak, or turns from sin and is reconciled with God.

Confession is an important part of that process, but only part of it. This reconciliation procedure entails an intimate conversion of one's heart prompted by God's grace, the confession of sins, the acceptance of a satisfaction or what we customarily call a penance, the absolution by a priest and the forgiveness, reconciliation and peace which follow these actions.

Penance thus is a more complete and accurate term which covers the confession of sins, but also includes the other elements vital to forgiveness and reconciliation. Calling this sacrament "confession" is not, therefore, erroneous, but it is inaccurate and inadequate.

Several weeks ago we spoke about modern man's forgetfulness of sin and the triple effects of sin. Through the Genesis story of Adam and Eve, we pointed out that sin weakens or destroys our friendship with God, disrupts our relationship with others and disturbs the world in which we live.

So, to be forgiven, to be at peace, we must be reconciled not only with God but with our neighbor and, to the extent possible, with the world around us.

To help us in that regard, the revised rite for Penance provides several different steps or procedures—whether we confess our sins alone or in a communal penance service.

First of all, a new form of absolution highlights the action of the Holy Spirit in forgiving us, the work of the Church in this process, and the reconciliation achieved through this sacrament.

> God, the Father of mercies,
> through the death and resurrection of his Son
> has reconciled the world to himself
> and sent the Holy Spirit among us
> for the forgiveness of sins:
> through the ministry of the Church
> may God give you pardon and peace,
> and I absolve you from your sins
> in the name of the Father, and of the Son,
> and of the Holy Spirit.

The Church also wants us to ponder seriously these words of Jesus which we find in St. Matthew's gospel:

> If you bring your gift to the altar and
> there recall that your brother has anything
> against you, leave your gift at the altar,
> go first to be reconciled with your brother,
> and then come and offer your gift. . . .

The Lord's Prayer has always been employed by the Church as a preparation for Holy Communion and as a petition for reconciliation. We ask God to give us our daily bread—which is both bread for our bodies and sacred bread for our hearts. But we also beg the Lord "to forgive us our trespasses as we forgive those who trespass against us."

The location of the Our Father at Mass is thus no accident. Before all of us share the same Body and Blood of Christ in Holy Communion, we first must make every effort to be reconciled, to be at peace with all men and women in the world. The Lord's Prayer helps us become aware of that and, at the same time, petition God for the courage to be forgiving.

It is for the same reason that the Church recommends we include the Our Father in every communal penance service.

Finally, the sign of peace is not really just a greeting, or a friendly handshake, or a kiss of love between family members. It may and should be all of those things. But more, it ought to be a sign of reconciliation, forgiveness, healing.

The persons in the pews around us—spouse, children, parents, friends, strangers—represent every individual in the world. They represent in a special way people against whom we have a grudge, about whom we are bitter, people we have not yet forgiven.

Our "Peace be with you" is then an act by which we empty out that bitterness, bury this grudge and forgive those who may have hurt us.

God's willingness to forgive us never ceases. But the Lord does put a price tag on this forgiveness. To be reconciled with God we must first be reconciled with one another. To regain peace with Jesus, we must reestablish peace in our hearts with others.

Christ's words about this are very clear and explicit:

"If you forgive the faults of others, your heavenly Father will forgive you yours. If you do not forgive others, neither will your Father forgive you."

OUTLINE OF HOMILY 2

Main thought: Just as sin breaks or weakens our relationship with God, one another and the world around us, so forgiveness and reconciliation mean we must be reconciled not only with God, but also with our neighbor and the world in which we live.

Aim for the congregation: I will recite the Our Father and give the sign of peace more conscious that forgiveness and peace from God depend upon my forgiveness of others.

I. INTRODUCTION

    Change from confession to penance and reconciliation
        —bulletin notice
        —pulpit announcement
    Reason for change
        —confession but a part of wider penance process
        —metanoia
        —reconciliation

II. BODY

    A. *Review of homily on sin*
        —Several weeks back
        —Triple effects of sin
        —So reconciliation involves those three aspects

    B. *Practical ways new rite brings this out*
        —Form of absolution (*TIP*, p. 70)
        —Matthew 5:21-26 (*TIP*, pp. 43-45)
        —Our Father
        —Sign of peace

III. CONCLUSION

        —Peace of Christ comes only with forgiveness of others
        —Matthew 6:14-15 (*TIP*, p. 45)

Homily 3

God's Good Words About Forgiveness

Early one morning Jesus came into the area around the Temple of Jerusalem, sat down and began to teach the crowds who flocked to hear him speak.

As he was doing so a group of religious leaders—scribes and Pharisees—who were hostile toward our Lord and jealous of him brought to Christ a woman who had been caught in adultery. They forced the poor woman, certainly embarrassed, probably with tears streaming down her face and fear in her eyes, to stand before Jesus. They then questioned the Lord:

"Teacher, this woman has been caught in the act of adultery. In the law, Moses ordered such women to be stoned. What do you have to say about the case?"

Inwardly they smiled to themselves, believing they had Jesus on the horns of a dilemma. If he said, "Stone her," his reputation as a loving, forgiving teacher and leader would be ruined. On the other hand, if he said, "Let her go," his reputation as a Jew and a faithful follower of the tradition of Moses would be destroyed.

Our Lord said nothing in response. Instead, he bent over and began to write something on the ground. Those are the only words we know Christ wrote and the winds or wear of time have long since erased them.

His questioners now became restless and pressed him again. "Should she be stoned or not?"

Jesus then straightened up and said to them: "Let the man among you who has no sin be the first to cast a stone at her."

He bent over and continued to write in silence.

First one person, an older individual left, next another, and another, and another until there were only two people remaining, Christ and the woman caught in adultery.

Our Lord stood up and said to her: "Woman, where did they all disappear to? Has no one condemned you?"

She whispered: "No one, sir."

Jesus then instructed the woman: "Nor do I condemn you. You may go. But from now on, avoid this sin."

This is not the only biblical story that speaks of Christ's mercy and forgiveness. There are over a dozen similar incidents in the gospels, events which either describe Jesus actually forgiving the repentant sinner or teaching about the mercy of God which has no limit and lasts forever.

Our Lord's own name, Jesus, means "savior," and he was given this title by an angel who explained that Mary's child had come to save people from their sins.

These passages from the bible surely do encourage and guide us. But the inspired word of scripture can accomplish even more for the Christian with a lively faith. We believe that God, Christ, is present in his holy word and personally speaks to us when we hear or read the sacred text.

It is for this reason that we proclaim these passages during Mass from a book which is large, impressive and dignified. That volume, called the lectionary, by itself speaks of the importance we give to sacred scripture in our worship.

It is for this reason also that in the new rite for the sacrament of Penance, the Church encourages us to read appropriate passages from the bible in our preparation for confession and provides an optional reading from scripture during the confession itself.

Reading a section or two from the bible beforehand or as part of the confession itself should help us to see our sins as Christ sees them, to sense deep in our hearts the need and to foster the desire to change, to be converted from our sinful ways, and to build up our confidence in God's loving mercy.

The new book, *Together in Peace,* is available at a table in the waiting area outside our room of reconciliation. You will find in it an easy procedure to help you prepare for the sacrament by reading selected passages from the bible. Whether you use the room or the confessional, whether you go face to face or anonymously, the minutes waiting will be well spent if you begin to make use of this booklet.

For those who go face to face and, at times, even for those who choose to confess in secret, the priest may likewise read for or with you a brief passage from the bible. He may also assign a passage from *Together in Peace* as the penance for your sins or at least as part of the satisfaction required.

While this may sound complicated or confusing, it actually is quite simple and should be very helpful. Perhaps the best way to begin might be to pick up *Together in Peace* the next time you come for this sacrament and follow its instructions.

In a congregation of our size over a weekend there probably is one person who has strayed from the Lord, who wishes to come home to the Father but feels afraid, or discouraged or wonders if God will forgive and take him or her back. The example of Jesus as he spoke with the woman caught in adultery should be encouraging to you. So, too, Christ's words ought to encourage you. "The son of man came to save sinners, not condemn them." "There is greater joy in heaven over one sinner who repents than over 99 just who need not repentance."

OUTLINE OF HOMILY 3

Main thought: In sacred scripture the Lord speaks to us many times about God's mercy and forgiveness.

Aim for the congregation: I will read a passage or two of scripture from this new book before my confession and expect the priest may use passages from the bible during my confession.

I. INTRODUCTION

Dramatization of story about woman taken in adultery (TIP, pp. 20-21)

II. BODY

    A. *Scriptural basis for God's mercy*
  —Not only one story, over a dozen similar ones
  —Meaning of Jesus, "savior"

    B. *Presence of Christ in scripture*
  —Words not only guide and encourage
  —Christ present (*Constitution on the Sacred Liturgy,* art. 7, see *TIP,* pp. 136-139)
  —Reason for dignified lectionary and use of the bible in the ritual

    C. *Use of scripture in the celebration of Penance*
  —Purpose (*TIP,* pp. 176, 179)
  —Use of *TIP* as preparation
  —Use of scripture during actual confession
  —Scripture passages as penances or satisfaction

III. CONCLUSION

  —Person in need of forgiveness and healing
  —Words of Jesus

Homily 4

Signs of Sorrow and Forgiveness

Lance Rentzel seemed to have everything in his favor: handsome, aggressive, college All-American, National Football League star, well known, married in the chapel of St. Patrick's Cathedral to a beautiful Hollywood personality, financially secure. . . . What more could an individual desire?

But Rentzel had a fatal flaw, a serious weakness which ruined much of this. Arrested in Minnesota on a morals charge involving a young child, he was, because of the bad publicity and the personal complications, traded by the Vikings to the Dallas Cowboys.

Soon, despite the great upset, his life resumed a somewhat normal pattern. But within a relatively short period he stumbled again. The same failure, the same weakness, the same arrest, but this time the matter was not so swiftly or easily resolved. He lost his position with the Cowboys, lost his wife, lost almost everything.

Both in desperation and through court order, Rentzel sought professional help and received psychiatric care. As part of his therapy, he wrote an autobiography, *When All the Laughter Died in Sorrow,* a painfully honest account of what happened in his life and why.

In the book he describes his second failure in Dallas, the next-day headlines, his apology to the football team and their acceptance of him as a person.

The Cowboys had assembled for a practice session, a strategy discussion for the next game. Rentzel began:

"I suppose you've all heard a lot of stories about me in the last few days, and I feel you should hear from me what's going on. Well, the stories are pretty much true, and I want you to understand the truth about it, so that you'll know how to handle it. . . . I guess everybody makes mistakes in his life. Well, I've made some bad ones. I'm in serious trouble and I don't know what's going to happen."

I got that much out without too much difficulty; then I began to choke badly. But for the first time they were seeing the real me. They were witnessing emotions that I really felt, but rarely expressed. It was not a prepared speech, I was just speaking from the heart; a few minutes, that's all I wanted to take, but it got so I was not sure I could finish.

"I want to apologize to you. If I've embarrassed you as teammates, I'm really sorry. I hope that you'll want me to stay on the team, and that you'll support me and consider me a friend—because that's all I want to be. That's what I want above all."

I sat down and there was not a sound for a second or two, then a few loud swallows, including my own. I sat there with my head down, feeling too ashamed to look at anyone. I wanted to crawl away and hide; I wanted this to be over. I was twenty-seven years old and I was supposed to be a responsible person. I was supposed to be a man with ambitions and big dreams, and all of a sudden I was a miserable idiot with a tremendous contempt for himself.

I started to cry, I couldn't help it, I fought it, holding my hand in front of my mouth. I looked up and saw that I wasn't the only one in tears. I wanted to run from the room, I began wishing Landry would turn out the damn lights and start the film so I could hide in the darkness, and it seemed like forever before they did.

Then, in the dark, Landry tried to bring everyone's attention back to the game, to watch the Green Bay kicking teams on film, but you could feel how impossible that was, I'd ruined that for the moment at least. Then this incredible thing happened: a hand grabbed my shoulder, a huge hand, and it held on, firmly, supportively, and then, from the other side, a tap on the arm, then again. The room was dark and the coach was talking, but there was a shuffling and a sound of scraping chairs, as one after another they moved to make contact with me. They wanted to remain anonymous and did not wish to be open about it, but they wanted to convey the unspoken message: "We're with you." I wondered how I could have doubted them. I knew one thing: I'd never forget that moment.

The meeting ended and the team went to dinner. The guys at my table talked normally, as they always did the night before a game. At times I forgot the trouble I was in and talked as if nothing had happened. Dan

Reeves came up and whispered, "Everyone makes a mistake, but few people have the courage to stand up and admit it the way you did. We're all on your side." During the rest of the meal, other players and coaches approached me; each came alone and said something in his own way to let me know he was not judging me. They understood what I was going through and they felt for me. And now, for the first time, these men who hardly ever weaken or display their feelings were saying things they ordinarily wouldn't.*

This story of a fallen football star may appear strange for a homily. However, I think it speaks to us through a powerful contemporary incident about one person's act of contrition and the touching, forgiving, accepting response of others to his expression of sorrow.

Roman Catholics have been making acts of contrition for years. But in the recent past this expression of sorrow for sins during confession has had a varied career. Many of us grew up with the practice of mumbling, "O my God I am heartily sorry," while the priest pronounced the words of absolution in Latin. Since most did not understand the phrases he proclaimed, it made little difference whether we heard or listened to them.

When the formula for absolution was changed into the vernacular a decade or so ago we began instead to listen to those words, "I absolve you from your sins. . . ." The act of contrition, we were told, should be said by ourselves beforehand.

With the new rite of Penance, we now make a slight shift. The Church wishes us to express our sorrow within the confession itself. The priest, however, is to wait until we do so, then pronounce the formula of forgiveness in English. We say "Amen" after he finishes.

What words of contrition or sorrow do we use? The old "O my God" is fine. A few words of your own are also perfectly acceptable. For those who wish a fresh start, some variety or a little help, the revised rite provides ten different acts of contrition from which you may choose. If you confess in the reconciliation room, you could even read one of these texts.

Our young boys and girls preparing for First Penance were and will be asked to learn one of these acts of contrition. They need to have a prayer like this memorized which can stay with them in the years ahead. Daily repetition of such a formula should deepen and perfect the inner attitude of

---

*From *When All the Laughter Died in Sorrow* by Lance Rentzel. Copyright © 1972 by Lance Rentzel. Reprinted by permission of the publishers, Saturday Review Press/E. P. Dutton Co., Inc.

sorrow we as Christians ought to have constantly in our hearts.

Here is the act of contrition our young people are learning:

> My God,
> I am sorry for my sins with all my heart.
> In choosing to do wrong
> and failing to do good,
> I have sinned against you
> whom I should love above all things.
> I firmly intend, with your help,
> to do penance,
> to sin no more,
> and to avoid whatever leads me to sin.
> Our Savior Jesus Christ
> suffered and died for us.
> In his name, my God, have mercy.

Lance Rentzel told teammates he was sorry. They responded by saying, "We understand, we accept your apology, we support you and are with you even though we don't approve of what you did."

However, they expressed their forgiveness and acceptance more in actions than in words. One by one the big, strong players moved to make contact with him, to touch him. As he said: "A hand grabbed my shoulder, a huge hand, and it held on, firmly, supportively, and then, from the other side, a tap on the arm, then again."

In the early Christian days, sinners were reconciled to the Church in a somewhat similar way. The bishop or his delegate, the priest, indicated the sinner had been received back into the Church by imposing hands upon the penitent Christian.

The Church today restores this practice as an option in the rite. It directs the priest to extend his hands over the penitent's head or at least to extend his right hand over or toward the penitent as he pronounces the words of absolution.

This, of course, can be done rather easily in a reconciliation room. In the customary confessional, the extension of both hands over a penitent's head will obviously be impossible and the extension of the right hand will normally not be visible to the penitent.

Moreover, each priest will develop his own style and vary the approach to meet the needs of different penitents.

The important part here is to recognize in the gesture a sign of forgiveness, healing and reconciliation. Whether it is one hand or both, only extended over or actually imposed upon your head, whether you receive it kneeling, standing or sitting, whether you can see the action or not—the gesture means our Lord has heard your act of contrition, accepts you back, forgives you, much as Lance Rentzel's teammates heard his apology and accepted him.

OUTLINE OF HOMILY 4

Main thought: The new rite of Penance provides an opportunity for the penitent to express his or her contrition and receive a sign of forgiveness and reconciliation.

Aim: I will be prepared to either read or say an act of contrition and have the priest show in some way that I have been forgiven and am reconciled.

I. INTRODUCTION

   Story of Lance Rentzel's sorrow and acceptance (When All the Laughter Died in Sorrow, New York, 1972, Bantam Books, Inc. pp. 13-15)

II. BODY

   A. *Act of Contrition*
      —History of contrition in rite of Penance
      —Pre-vernacular, vernacular
      —Present recommendation (*TIP,* p. 68)
      —Options (*TIP,* pp. 68-70)
      —Possibilities in reconciliation room
      —First Penance: children and memorization (*TIP,* p. 68)

   B. *Sign of Forgiveness and Reconciliation*
      —Basis in history
      —New rite's direction (*TIP,* pp. 70, 144-146, 177)
      —Variety of implementation

III. CONCLUSION

   —Ritual contrition and forgiveness linked with Rentzel's sorrow and acceptance

Homily 5

A Sacrament for Growth

Here is the hypothetical confession of a married man:
"Forgive me, Father, I'm a married man. It's been a month since my last confession. I got angry and lost my temper at the children. This happens often now when I get home from work. I'm tired and I don't want to be bothered.

"I know this is selfish. My anger just makes things worse. I'll try to spend more time with the kids and listen to them instead of yell. Where should I start? Have you any advice?"

Does that sound like your confession?
In the past ten years there has been a general decline in the number of persons who receive the sacrament of Penance and in the frequency with which Catholic people confess their sins.

At the same time many individuals are a little uneasy about this pattern in their lives. They feel somewhat guilty about not going to confession, yet don't really want to confess, believe they get little out of the sacrament, and see almost no improvement as a result of the experience.

They normally don't confess like the married man in our sample. Instead, their confession becomes almost a grocery list of the same sins, for which they receive the same penance, and afterwards continue to sin in the same way. They confess as they did in the eighth grade.

The married man's confession, on the other hand, was not really a necessary one. There were no serious sins mentioned which required the sacrament. He did not *have* to go. We might call it instead a devotional confession, one designed to help him grow as a person.

His confession contained an answer to three basic questions: What did I do? Why did I do it? How can I be better? That approach can help turn a routine confession of sins into a sacrament which leads to great personal growth.

First, the question: What did I do?

Bishop Topel of Spokane has made some remarkable changes in his life as a bishop in the last few years—he sold his episcopal palace and moved into a modest center-city apartment; he cultivates a small garden and cooks his own food; he drives a well-used car and on weekends helps out priests who are ill.

He attributes his change in life-style to frequent use of the sacrament of Penance. Bishop Topel told a group of liturgists at a recent conference the kinds of sins he now confesses: failure to love as Christ does, failure to trust enough in the Lord, failure to be properly grateful for God's gifts.

The new ritual for Penance contains an examination of conscience which might help us discover some areas we have not usually considered as matter for confession, failures similar to those mentioned by Bishop Topel.

Under the Lord's command to "love the Lord your God with your whole heart," it asks questions like these:

> Is my heart set on God, so that I really love him above all things and am faithful to his commandments, as a son loves his father? Or am I more concerned about the things of this world?

> Have I prayed morning and evening? When I pray, do I really raise my mind and heart to God or is it a matter of words only?

Under Jesus' command to "love one another as I have loved you," it inquires:

> Have I a genuine love for my neighbor? Or do I use them for my own ends, or do to them what I would not want done to myself?

> Do I share my possessions with the less fortunate? Do I do my best to help the victims of oppression, misfortune, and poverty? Or do I look down on my neighbor, especially the poor, the sick, the elderly, strangers, and people of other races?

If I have been injured, have I been ready to make peace, for the love of Christ, and to forgive, or do I harbor hatred and the desire for revenge?

Finally, under Christ's directive to "be perfect as your Father is perfect," it raises these issues:

Where is my life really leading me? Is the hope of eternal life my inspiration? Have I tried to grow in the life of the Spirit through prayer, reading the word of God and meditating on it, receiving the sacraments, self-denial? Have I been anxious to control my vices, my bad inclinations and passions? Have I been proud and boastful, thinking myself better in the sight of God and despising others as less important than myself? Have I imposed my own will on others, without respecting their freedom and rights?

What use have I made of time, of health, and strength, of the gifts God has given me to be used like the talents in the gospel? Do I use them to become more perfect every day? Or have I been lazy and too much given to leisure?

What did I do is an important question, of course. But why did I do it is the more critical one.
The married man in our sample tried to get beneath the surface and discover the cause for his anger with the children.
So, too, in our own lives what we do may indicate an evilness in our heart or may be the result of some quite different factors.
For example, if I am sharp, angry or nasty in the morning to another person, those words and actions may express a dislike or hatred for that individual or may simply reflect my headache or sleepless night or preoccupation with a heavy problem.
If we confess every few months, it might be better to make then a general review of that period and evaluate our basic dispositions or attitudes rather than draw up a lengthy list of lesser sins committed. We thus are getting behind the action and going to the real heart of the matter.

The final question, how can I be better, looks to the future instead of the past.
The priest's advice can help in this regard, of course, but the Church

also would like the penitent to perform penances which are in some way connected with the sins confessed. In that fashion there is an additional carry-over from the sacrament into one's daily life. The penance thus can aid in healing wounds and in overcoming weaknesses caused by the sins.

The best kind of these personal, creative penances are those developed by the penitent on his or her own.

One confessor asked a little girl what she might do to make up with her mother for a misdeed.

> She replied: "Bake a cake."
> "Would that please your mother?"
> "Yes."
> "Can you bake a cake?"
> "Yes."
> "All right, for your penance bake a cake for your mother."

When you think about the mess in the kitchen she would make, you wonder if it would be a penance for the child or for the mother.

In some instances, the priest may assign as a penance a scriptural passage from *Together in Peace,* and even read it with the penitent before giving absolution.

For example, a person who confesses undue anxiety or worry about a current problem or future development might have this biblical text given as a penance:

> If God can clothe in such splendor the grass of the field, which blooms today and is thrown on the fire tomorrow, will he not provide much more for you, O weak in faith! Stop worrying, then, over questions like, "What are we to eat, or what are we to drink, or what are we to wear?" The unbelievers are always running after these things. Your heavenly Father knows all that you need. Seek first his kingship over you, his way of holiness, and all these things will be given you besides. Enough, then, of worrying about tomorrow. Let tomorrow take care of itself. Today has troubles enough of its own.

Our experience with the youngsters preparing for First Penance indicates they can grasp in their own way this notion of what did I do, why did I do it, how can I be better.

To conclude, here is another sample confession, this time of a fourth grade girl:

> Help me, Father, to make a good confession. I'm a fourth grade girl and it has been three months since my last confession.
>
> I have a brother in the second grade and we are always getting into fights and then my mom and dad get mad at us. I think I fight with him so much because I feel he's my dad's favorite and I'm jealous of him. I'm going to try to think more about the attention that dad gives to me and forget about noticing all the attention that my brother gets.
>
> I am sorry for this sin and will try to change my attitude toward my brother.

OUTLINE OF HOMILY 5

Main thought: The sacrament of Penance is not merely for reconciliation with God when we have been totally cut off from the Lord, but also a means of helping us grow into the kind of persons we should become.

Aim: I will strive to receive the sacrament of Penance at least every three months and keep in mind: What did I do? Why did I do it? How can I be better?

I. INTRODUCTION

—*Sample confession of married man* (*TIP*, p. 72 A)

II. BODY

Experience of past years
—Anxiety about decline in use of the sacrament
—Problem of routine

A. *What did I do?*
—Bishop Topel
—Examination of Conscience (*TIP*, pp. 54-58)

B. *Why did I do it?*
—Relationship of acts and attitudes
—Review of dispositions

C. *How can I be better?*
—Penance linked with sin confessed
—Penance for a child
—Scriptural passage—trust (*TIP*, pp. 52-53, Matthew 6:19-34)

III. CONCLUSION

—Possibility of young doing this
—Sample of fourth-grade girl (*TIP*, p. 72 B)

Homily 6

Together in Peace

On Palm Sunday afternoon at 5:00 o'clock, 400 persons came to Holy Family Church in a small upstate New York city for a communal or common penance service.

Announcements from the pulpits of three area parishes and publicity in the local press stressed that, because the service itself has the power to inspire and guide, the ten priests hearing confessions would ask few, if any, questions and give little or no advice.

The first 20 minutes of the service included congregational singing, readings from the bible, a homily, a common examination of conscience, a litany of contrition and the Our Father. Then the priests, vested in white albs and purple stoles, left the altar for the various confessional places.

During the next 45 minutes almost everyone in the church went to confession. During that lengthy period the congregation sang a song, prayed or reflected in silence, recited a common prayer, then again prayed in silence, listened to the choir sing an appropriate song, again reflected in silence. This pattern was repeated throughout the confession session.

The people prayed not just for themselves, but for those others who were actually in or about to enter the confessional. There was a common concern for one another, hoping each person would have the faith and courage needed for a real conversion experience which brings such peace.

At the end the priests returned to the sanctuary, all joined in a song of joyful praise and the main celebrant gave a final blessing to the congregation.

Why hold such a service?

It brings out more clearly that as Christians we form a community or a family and what helps or hurts one member, helps or hurts the entire family or community. When one person sins, the whole community suffers or is weakened. When one person repents and becomes reconciled with God, the whole Christian family becomes stronger and rejoices.

The benefits of such a communal penance celebration are expressed in these more technical words of the new ritual for Penance.

> Communal celebration shows more clearly the ecclesial nature of penance. The faithful listen together to the word of God, which proclaims his mercy and invites them to conversion; at the same time they examine the conformity of their lives with that word of God and help each other through common prayer. After each person has confessed his sins and received absolution, all praise God together for his wonderful deeds on behalf of the people he has gained for himself through the blood of his Son.

As Catholic Christians we believe that our Lord and thus his Spirit is present in many ways when we come together. When we pray in common, he is there; when we listen to the bible, he speaks to us; when we help or forgive another, he is present; when we receive Holy Communion, or participate in Mass, or receive any of the sacraments, Christ comes into our midst.

This presence of Jesus and his Spirit in our midst has the power of forgiving our sins. Thus, when we gather for a communal penance service, the readings, prayers, common concern and mutual forgiveness can in themselves bring about the forgiveness of our sins. Serious sins, of course, require perfect love in our hearts for their forgiveness outside the sacrament of Penance; they must also be confessed at the first opportunity.

But it might be good for us to remember, however, that these common celebrations do have the power within themselves to forgive our sins without the sacrament of Penance.

Some priests and penitents find the type of communal service at Holy Family we described in the beginning of this homily rather frustrating and impersonal.

The priest is limited in what he can say after the confession of sins; the penitent feels the pressure to be brief and not to seek individual counsel or assistance.

A second communal celebration, similar, but different, tries to resolve that problem. It is an open-ended kind of service.

The first part is exactly like the one we outlined—readings, prayers, the Lord's Prayer and so on. Just before the priests leave the sanctuary for the confessions, however, the congregation is told something like this:

"If you would like simply to sit here and reflect on the peace and reconciliation you experience as a result of this service, please do so. There will be some suitable music in the background to help you with that prayerful reflection."

"If you would like to continue this celebration of forgiveness and joy downstairs afterwards, please join us there for coffee and cookies."

"If you would like the personal, individual meeting with Christ which comes in a unique way through the sacrament of Penance, the priests will be available in several locations as long as you need them."

In this type of service there is not the joyful coming together at the end for a common song and final blessing. That is its weakness. But there is no time pressure on priest or penitent during the confession itself and that is its strength.

A young married man in his 30's remarked after the Palm Sunday communal celebration at Holy Family: "That really helped me get to confession. To see all those people stand up and head for the different priests gave me the courage to do the same."

The congregation that day sang the concluding song with great joy and unusual enthusiasm. It really should be no surprise they did.

When we have something in our eye, when our back hurts, when our head or a tooth aches, we feel bad all over. But when we get the speck out of our eye, when the back clears up, when the headache or toothache disappears, we feel good all over.

When a single sinner returns to God, there is great joy in heaven and on earth; when many sinners return, that joy is enormous.

"I tell you, there will likewise be more joy in heaven over one repentant sinner than over ninety-nine righteous people who have no need to repent."

OUTLINE OF HOMILY 6

Main thought: Communal penance services help a Christian become aware that the whole Church or Body of Christ is weakened by an individual's sin and strengthened by that person's conversion and reconciliation.

Aim: I will participate in one of these communal penance services the next time it is celebrated in the parish.

I. INTRODUCTION

   Holy Family Palm Sunday experience

II. BODY

   A. *Value of Communal Penance Service*
   —Family or community strengthened and weakened by sin and conversion
   —Various benefits of communal services (*TIP*, p. 178)

   B. *Power of God's Presence in Forgiving*
   —Various ways Christ is present (*TIP*, pp. 136-139)
   —Power of Holy Spirit to forgive
   —Serious sins

   C. *Two Kinds of Celebrations*
   —Frustrations in service described
   —Open-ended celebration
   —Strength and weakness of both

III. CONCLUSION

   —Observations—person present, concluding song
   —Comparison to human body
   —Scriptural quote (Luke 15:1-7, *TIP*, pp. 64-65)

Material for the Weekly Bulletin

The paragraphs which follow are designed for use in the weekly bulletin on a regular or occasional basis over, obviously, a lengthy period of time. They are categorized according to the topics covered by the six model homilies. However, they need not be employed in the order given, although normally they should be inserted after the pertinent subject has been treated from the pulpit.

A paragraph introducing the next weekend's topic is included for each of the six homilies. Our experience has indicated this is a most effective practice both for building interest in the forthcoming sermon and in conveying to the congregation the advance planning which has gone into the preaching process.

1. SIN

Preceding week: Do you think our society has lost its sense of sin? Are we inclined to explain away everything, rationalize our failures, justify the cutting of moral corners? Next weekend at all the Masses we will look into these issues and begin a series of homilies explaining the new rite of Penance.

Related material for follow-up:

1. Dr. Karl Menninger, the famous psychiatrist, has this to say about sin, modern man and a sense of personal responsibility:

> My proposal is for the revival or reassertion of personal responsibility in all human acts, good and bad. Not total responsibility, but not zero either. I believe that all evildoing in which we become involved to any

degree tends to evoke guilt feelings and depression. These may or may not be clearly perceived, but they affect us. They may be reacted to and covered up by all kinds of escapism, rationalization, and reaction or symptom formation. To revive the half-submerged idea of personal responsibility and to seek appropriate measures of reparation might turn the tide of our aggressions and of the moral struggle in which much of the world population is engaged.*

2. Many of us whose religious training dates back before the Second Vatican Council tended to think of sin almost exclusively in terms of God and myself, Jesus and me. In this view sin offended God and left a mark on my soul. Confession washed away that sin and made me friends with God again. There is, of course, much truth in this approach, but a fuller understanding of sin leads us to see that sin also disrupts my relationship with other human beings and upsets the world in which we live.

3. Why has there been a drastic drop in confessions over the past ten years? There is no one reason to explain this. Reaction to bad earlier experiences with the sacrament, an awareness that confession is not required before Communion, concern about routine reception of Penance without real improvement are some of the explanations given. But loss of a sense of sin is certainly a significant factor. Unless I believe I am a sinner and have sinned, it is very unlikely I will approach Jesus as my Savior or seek to meet him in faith through the sacrament of Penance.

4. Once again we turn to Dr. Menninger for some advice in today's world. He tells priests, ministers and rabbis they should preach about sin more often:

> Some clergymen prefer pastoral counseling of individuals to the pulpit function. But the latter is a greater opportunity to both heal and prevent. An ounce of prevention is worth a pound of cure, indeed, and there is much prevention to be done for large numbers of people who hunger and thirst after direction toward righteousness. Clergymen have a golden opportunity to prevent some of the accumulated misapprehensions, guilt, aggressive action, and other roots of later mental suffering and mental disease.
>
> How? Preach! Tell it like it is. Say it from the pulpit. Cry it

---

*Reprinted by permission of Hawthorn Books, Inc. from *Whatever Became of Sin?* by Karl Menninger, M.D., p. 178. Copyright © 1973 by Karl Menninger, M.D. All rights reserved.

from the housetops.

What shall we cry?

Cry comfort, cry repentance, cry hope. Because recognition of our part in the world transgression is the only remaining hope.*

2. RECONCILIATION

Preceding week: Next weekend we will explain why the new ritual for confession is called the order of Penance or Rite of Reconciliation. The homily, our second in the series preparing for this change, will also cover the sign of peace, a gesture which in the beginning confused many and still troubles some.

1. A wise and holy Benedictine monk frequently reminded troubled sinners and anxious persons who came to him that God's love never ceases. We can close ourselves off from that love, but the love never stops. Thus, with the conversion of a sinner it is more the Lord's grace than the person's efforts which brings about this needed change. Christ's loving grace works to soften and convert our sinful hearts. When we finally respond, God's forgiving grace welcomes us home.

2. The new formula of absolution in the sacrament of Penance teaches us that the risen Jesus working in the Holy Spirit through the ministry of the Church reconciles us with the Father, with one another and the world around us. Our "Amen" at the end indicates we believe this.

> God, the Father of mercies,
> through the death and resurrection of his Son
> has reconciled the world to himself
> and sent the Holy Spirit among us
> for the forgiveness of sins;
> through the ministry of the Church
> may God give you pardon and peace,
> and I absolve you from your sins
> in the name of the Father, and of the Son,
> and of the Holy Spirit.

3. The sign of peace has been a part of worship for centuries going back even before Christ's time. The Jewish phrase, "Shalom," expressed

---
*Ibid., p. 228

a hope that all of God's blessings and peace would come to the person greeted. The Church took this over immediately for Christian worship and first placed it after the homily before the gifts were brought forward. However, soon it moved to the present spot—after the Lord's Prayer and before Communion. We ask God in the Our Father to forgive us as we forgive others; we join with others at Communion in eating the same Body of Christ. These words and this gesture demand we be at peace with one another.

    4. There is no peace for the unforgiving person. Regardless of how deep the hurt, how cruel the deed, how unjust the action, we never will know peace unless we forgive those who have hurt, mistreated or injured us. Jesus on the cross is our model here. The innocent one forgiving the guilty.

3. GOD'S GOOD WORDS ABOUT FORGIVENESS

Preceding week: We never tire of hearing or preaching about God's loving mercy and forgiveness. Do you? Next weekend our third homily preparing for the new rite of Penance or reconciliation will consider the forgiving words of Jesus we find in the bible. It will explain how these should occupy a larger part in the process we will follow when receiving this sacrament in the future.

    1. The *Constitution on the Sacred Liturgy* directed the experts who would revise our worship services to open up the treasures of the bible more lavishly that "richer fare may be provided for the faithful at the table of God's word." In this way we should develop a "warm and living love for scripture." We believe that Christ "is present in his word, since it is he himself who speaks when the holy Scriptures are read in the church." These are the reasons for the increased use of the bible in the revised rite of Penance.

    2. The Church tells us in its directions for the new ritual of Penance: "Through the word of God the Christian receives light to recognize his sins and is called to conversion and to confidence in God's mercy." The scriptural readings also illustrate for us "the voice of God calling men back to conversion and ever closer conformity with Christ; the mystery of our reconciliation through the death and resurrection of Christ and through the gift of the Holy Spirit; the judgment of God about good and evil in men's lives as a help in the examination of conscience."

    3. In the pamphlet rack and near our confessionals are copies of a new book, *Together in Peace*. It contains over 70 scriptural passages which

speak about God's love and forgiveness. The text has a simple process to help you celebrate more effectively the sacrament of Penance. We hope penitents will pick up the booklet as they prepare for their confession and read through the steps given. It will take but a few moments and should enrich your experience with this sacrament of peace.

4. After the opening prayers of your confession, the priest may either read or recite from memory a passage from the bible, even inviting you to join with him as he does so. Here is a typical one the priest could use:

> It is precisely in this that God proves his love for us: that while we were still sinners, Christ died for us. Now that we have been justified by his blood, it is all the more certain that we shall be saved by him from God's wrath. Romans 5:8-9.

4. SIGNS OF SORROW AND FORGIVENESS

Preceding week: Our homilies of preparation for the new rite of Penance continue next weekend with an explanation of the topic, "Signs of Sorrow and Forgiveness." It will feature a story about a famous football player's failure, his act of contrition and his teammates' gestures of forgiveness.

1. The Church as a pilgrim church looking forward to a kingdom which is already, but not yet, constantly needs to renew, update and reform itself. We must then expect change as a very part of the Church's nature. But we want only change which means progress and growth, not change for the sake of change. The Church's directive that we now express our sorrow with an act of contrition during confession itself (not just before) is one of those carefully thought-out changes which should help us grow and derive richer spiritual results from the sacrament of Penance.

2. The old "O my God, I am heartily sorry" act of contrition is perfectly acceptable in the new rite for Penance. A brief expression of sorrow for sin in your own words likewise fulfills the requirement indicated by the revised regulations. For those who wish some variety, a fresh start or a little help, the ritual gives ten acts of contrition which can be read or memorized. Here is a sample of one contained in the book, *Together in Peace:*

> Lord Jesus, Son of God,
> have mercy on me, a sinner.

3. The revised rituals published by the Holy See since Vatican II include a gesture of touch for most of the sacraments. Priest, parents and godparents make the sign of the cross on the baptized person's forehead; the celebrant imposes hands upon the person to be confirmed or the ill patient to be anointed; the bishop extends his hands on the head of a man about to be ordained; those around the bed of the dying are encouraged to sign the sick person's forehead as a reminder of Baptism. Similarly, in the sacrament of Penance the priest extends both or at least the right hand over or toward the penitent, indicating in a visible, sensible way God has given forgiveness and welcomes the sinner home.

4. Should the young memorize an act of contrition? We think so. Prayer must come from the heart, but a formula learned in early years and repeated daily can help foster the proper attitudes which we should have in our hearts. It also clarifies for us those deep, but often unclear feelings about our past sins and failures. However, neither the young nor old should be anxious about reciting a memorized prayer in confession itself. Any expression of contrition will do there. Nevertheless, reciting on our lips or in our hearts an act of contrition every day has real value for a person's spiritual life.

5. A SACRAMENT FOR GROWTH

Preceding week: Next weekend we will speak on Penance as "A sacrament for growth." This fifth in our series of explanatory homilies on the new rite will look at three questions: What did I do? Why did I do it? How can I be better?

1. How often should I go to confession? A good question which does not permit a mathematical answer. We only *have* to confess, the Church tells us, when we totally cut ourselves off from God by a serious (mortal) sin. But we also only *have* to receive Communion once a year during Easter time. Yet the Church encourages us to communicate frequently, even daily. In general we should receive the sacrament of Penance whenever we can do so with faith and a sense of inner conversion. That will be more frequent for some than for others. Perhaps a good thumb rule for the ordinary Catholic is about every three months or four times a year, like the old ember days of spring, summer, fall and winter.

2. Faith is the key element behind every sacrament in the Catholic Church. We need faith to recognize Jesus beneath the signs and symbols of

our worship. The liturgy is essentially a meeting with Christ in faith. Sometimes our faith overflows into our feelings, but not necessarily. We can experience our Lord through faith in the sacrament of Penance even when on a particular occasion we don't "feel" anything. The fact is we often do feel much better following a confession of sins, but it is unwise to measure its effectiveness for us by the good feeling afterwards.

    3. One way of overcoming routine in so-called "devotional confessions" is by concentrating on the what, why and how in a few areas of concern rather than drawing up a list of the lesser sins committed. In this way we try to evaluate our overall attitude or disposition and see how this can be changed or improved. The book we have available, *Together in Peace,* offers some suggestions for looking at a dozen of these areas of concern which you might find helpful. Pick one or two each time you prepare for the sacrament.

    4. The Church today, as in the past, sees the desirability of creative and personal penances in place of or as a complement to the traditional Our Fathers and Hail Marys. It seeks acts of satisfaction which bear a close link with the sins confessed and can thus serve as something of a carry-over into the penitent's future life. Reading an appropriate scriptural passage is one such penance. Here is another: For unkind and uncharitable words about another: mention good points about that person to others or pray for the individual offended.

6.   TOGETHER IN PEACE

Preceding weekend: Next weekend we will conclude our preparation for the new rite of Penance by considering a very recent, but rapid, development in the Church: communal or common penance services.

    1. The homily in a communal penance service, according to the new rite, should:

> Remind the faithful that sin works against God, against the community and one's neighbors, and against the sinner himself. Therefore, it would be good to recall:
>
>   a) the infinite mercy of God, greater than all our sins, by which again and again he calls us back to himself;
>
>   b) the need for interior repentance, by which we are genuinely prepared to make reparation for sin;

  c) the social aspect of grace and sin, by which the actions of individuals in some degree affect the whole body of the Church;
  d) the duty to make satisfaction for sin, which is effective because of Christ's work of reparation and requires especially, in addition to the works of penance, the exercise of true charity toward God and neighbor.

  2. Will confession soon be a practice of the past for Roman Catholics? Will we have general absolution without having to confess our sins individually to the priest? Not really. The new ritual does provide for special occasions when penitents can be given absolution without confession. However, those situations are limited and even when this does occur the person with serious sins has the obligation to confess them at the first opportunity to a priest in the traditional manner.
  3. Individual auricular confession and communal penance services do not compete with, but instead complement, each other. For that reason in our parish we continue to have regularly scheduled hours for individual confession and, at the same time, plan frequent communal services. These will be celebrated during Advent and Lent and throughout the year at times to be announced. In addition, the priests are always available for individual confessions by appointment.
  4. The Introduction to the new rite contains these words which serve as a foundation for communal penance services:

"By a hidden and loving mystery of God's design men are joined together in the bonds of supernatural solidarity, so much so that the sin of one harms the others just as the holiness of one benefits the others." Penance always entails reconciliation with our brothers and sisters who are always harmed by our sins.
  In fact, men frequently join together to commit injustice. It is thus only fitting that they should help each other in doing penance so that freed from sin by the grace of Christ they may work with all men of good will for justice and peace in the world.

HANDOUTS

The material in this section may be reproduced in any way for distribution to parishioners after Masses on appropriate weekends.

Rite for Reconciliation of Individual Penitents

1. Reception of the Penitent
After the priest warmly welcomes and kindly greets the penitent, both together make the sign of the cross.

The priest then prays for the penitent who, at the end, answers: *Amen.*

2. Reading of the Word of God
The priest either from memory or by reading may, if the situation is suitable, recite a passage of Scripture which speaks about God's mercy or calls us to conversion and a change of heart.

When circumstances permit, he may invite the penitent to read the text with him.

3. Confession of Sins and Acceptance of Satisfaction
The penitent confesses his or her sins; the priest, after discussing with the penitent his or her spiritual state and giving appropriate counsel, assigns an act of penance or satisfaction.

4. Prayer of Penitent and Absolution
The penitent expresses sorrow for sin by reciting the traditional formula, one of the ten new prayers given, or similar personal words of contrition.

The priest then extends his hands over the penitent's head (or at least extends his right hand) and pronounces the formula of absolution.

The penitent listens prayerfully and, at the conclusion, responds: *Amen.*

5. Proclamation of Praise of God and Dismissal
The priest says:
Give thanks to the Lord, for he is good.
The penitent concludes:
His mercy endures forever.

The priest then dismisses the penitent with a prayer or suitable phrase and the penitent responds: *Amen* or *Thank you.*

Communal Penance Services
(Rite for Reconciliation of Several Penitents with Individual Confession and Absolution)

1. Introductory Rites
An *entrance song* is sung while the priest enters the church to help develop a sense of community and properly dispose the congregation.

The priest *greets* the congregation and gives a brief *explanation* of the service.

The priest then invites the community to *pray* in *silence* for a short period and, afterwards, *prays out loud* in its name.

The congregation responds *Amen* to this prayer.

2. Celebration of the Word of God
One or several *readings* interspersed with a song, a psalm or reflective silence begin this part of the rite.

There follows a *homily* based on the texts of the readings and designed to lead penitents to examine their consciences and renew their lives.

All present then spend some time in making an *examination of conscience* and arousing true sorrow for sins. A leader may help in this regard.

3. Rite of Reconciliation
All kneel or bow and make a *general confession of sins.* The congregation then stands and says or sings an *appropriate litany* or *song.*

All say together the *Our Father.*

Penitents make their *individual confession,* receive a penance or satisfaction and are absolved. The other parts of individual confession are omitted in these services.

Priests and penitents stand and offer *praise for God's mercy,* usually through a suitable song.

The celebrant concludes with a *common prayer* to which the people say: *Amen.*

4. Concluding Rite
The priest bestows several *final blessings* with the people responding *Amen* after each.

A leader *dismisses* the congregation with a phrase like: *The Lord has freed you from your sins. Go in peace.*

All answer: *Thanks be to God.*

How to Use Together in Peace

For immediate preparation and use with the sacrament of Penance, *Together in Peace** works in this manner:

Step 1: Prayer for Light and Courage

We begin with a brief prayer asking God to help us believe in his mercy, to see our sins just as they are, to confess them honestly despite the pain that involves, to experience his peace, and to change our future lives.

This prayer from the heart can be in your own words and thoughts or may be expressed in one of the formulas given in the text.

Step 2: God's Good Words About Forgiveness

The bible is filled with stories and teachings about God's limitless mercy, love and forgiveness. Read now one or a few selections from *Together in Peace* and reflect for several moments upon them.

Step 3: A Look Into the Heart

The text offers many suggestions to aid in examining our consciences. We seek to answer three questions: What did I do? Why did I do it? How can I be better?

Step 4: The Confession of Sin

Together in Peace contains the new rite for individual confession and two sample confessions as models for penitents.

Step 5: Penances for the Past and for the Future

The confessor imposes upon you a penance or satisfaction for your sins as the final step in this sacrament of reconciliation. Designed to repair the harm done and to heal the wounds caused by these misdeeds, it is also intended to help you improve in the days ahead. He will, as your penance, assign a prayer or prayers, propose some action related to a particular sin confessed, or designate one, perhaps several of the readings given in *Together in Peace.* The priest may even offer to read with you the biblical passage selected before pronouncing the words of absolution and forgiveness.

---

*At home this text may serve as a daily prayer book or meditation manual. Many have discovered psalms, readings or prayers they find particularly helpful and read them frequently. Those who use it in that way are really making remote preparations for the sacrament of Penance. *(Together in Peace,* Penitent's Edition. Ave Maria Press. Notre Dame, Ind., 46556. $1.35)